HOLY GHOST

Who you know is more important than what you know

KAKRA BAIDEN

AIR POWER
PUBLICATIONS

Copyright © 2020 by Airpower Publishing, LLC

Holy Ghost
by Kakra Baiden

Printed in the United States of America

ISBN: 978-1-945123-19-1

All rights reserved. No part of this document may be reproduced or transmitted in any form, by any means (electronic, photocopying, recording, or otherwise) without the written permission of the author.

Unless otherwise indicated, Bible quotations are taken from the Holy Bible, New International Version®, NIV® Copyright © 1973, 1978, 1984, 2011 by Biblica, Inc.® Used by permission. All rights reserved worldwide.

Scripture marked KJV is taken from the King James Version of the Bible. Public domain.

Scripture marked NKJV is taken from the New King James Version® of the Bible. Copyright © 1982 by Thomas Nelson. Used by permission. All rights reserved.

Dedicated to Eastwood Anaba.

TABLE OF CONTENTS

Chapter 1	The Holy Ghost	1
Chapter 2	Two Ways to Experience the Holy Ghost	3
Chapter 3	You Must Be Able to Identify Him	8
Chapter 4	Relate to the Holy Ghost by One of His Forms	9
Chapter 5	The Holy Ghost Is the Ghost of Jesus	11
Chapter 6	See the Holy Ghost As Jesus	16
Chapter 7	Why Is It Important to Know the Holy Ghost?	19
Chapter 8	The Holy Ghost Is the Custodian	20
Chapter 9	The Marriage of Isaac and Sarah	22
Chapter 10	He Is the Custodian of God's Power	26
Chapter 11	He Is the Custodian of Spiritual and Ministry Gifts	29
Chapter 12	He Is the Custodian of God's Finances	32
Chapter 13	He Is the Custodian of Salvation	35
Chapter 14	You Need an Introduction	38
Chapter 15	You Must Talk to Him	40
Chapter 16	You Must Know Him	44
Chapter 17	You Need a Revelation of Him	46
Chapter 18	You Must Have the Same Nature	49
Chapter 19	You Must Share His Interests	53
Chapter 20	You Need the Gifts of the Spirit	55
Chapter 21	You Need to Fast and Pray	66
Final Words		71
About the Author		72

CHAPTER 1

THE HOLY GHOST

The Power of the Holy Ghost

THE ATMOSPHERE WAS electric and the congregation was expectant as Pastor Eastwood stood to preach. The sermon was fiery and powerful, and at the end of his sermon he announced, "The Holy Ghost is here."

Suddenly something like a wind seemed to blow over the congregation and the manifestations started. Sections of the congregation started falling under the power of God, some were crying, some shaking, screaming, etc. There seemed to be utter confusion as the power of God ignited the atmosphere. I was mesmerized, wowed by the whole experience.

I wondered, how come the Holy Ghost seemed to work with some people so easily? Why was I not seeing such manifestations in my life and ministry? It was like the Holy Spirit was responding to the pastor's commands.

My Hunger Was Stirred

I was about twenty-two years old and very hungry for the supernatural move of God. I had been ministering in small-group meetings but never experienced the power of God in this way. This was the trigger point of my hunger.

I said to myself, "Holy Ghost, I think I know very little about You and would like to know You more."

My pastor, Dag Heward-Mills, added fuel to this already blazing fire in my heart when he also started moving powerfully with great power and manifestations of the Holy Spirit. One day he showed me a video of another powerful man of God who operated in similar fashion. I saw this pastor clothed in a white suit, singing "Hallelujah."

After a while he said, "The Holy Ghost is here." A great wave seemed to sweep over the congregation and sections of the congregation fell under the power of God; miracles and healings were taking place all over. I knew the presence of God, but others seemed to know the manifest presence of God.

I used to think that God had chosen a few select group of people to use and I was not one of them. A particular Scripture changed my mindset. Peter went to preach to the Gentiles and he was shocked when the Holy Ghost filled them. He heard them speaking in tongues. "Then Peter began to speak: 'I now realize how true it is that God does not show favoritism but accepts from every nation the one who fears him and does what is right' " (Acts 10:34-35).

I learned that God had no favorites. We all have equal access to Him irrespective of age, gender, race, color, economics, education, or social status. He has only two requirements: you must fear Him; and you must be righteous. Based on this verse I knew that it was possible to take my relationship with the Holy Ghost to a higher level. This hunger made me embark on a quest to know Him, the Holy Ghost, the third Person of the Trinity.

CHAPTER 2

TWO WAYS TO EXPERIENCE THE HOLY GHOST

The Latent and the Manifest Presence of God

YOU CAN EXPERIENCE the Holy Ghost in two ways. The two ways are: the latent presence of God, and the manifest presence of God. Latent means present but not visible, and manifest means present and visible to the senses.

Towards the end of His life Jesus told His disciples He had to depart to heaven so the Holy Ghost could replace Him on the earth. He said: "And I will ask the Father, and he will give you another advocate to help you and be with you forever—the Spirit of truth. The world cannot accept him, because it neither sees him nor knows him. But you know him, for he lives with you and will be in you. I will not leave you as orphans; I will come to you" (John 14:16-18).

The two ways are: "He can be *in* you," which is the presence of God, or the latent presence of God; or "He can be *with* you," which is the manifest presence of God. Let's examine them a little bit more closely.

The Latent Presence of God

He Will Be in You

Some years ago I went to preach in a certain town and slept in a hotel. In the morning I observed someone had taken a bite of the loaf of bread I brought. Immediately I knew mice were in the room although I had not seen any. Their presence was not manifest; it was latent.

The word "in" suggests something internal and invisible. When you become born again the Holy Ghost comes to live in you. Paul said to the new believers in the church of Corinth, "Know ye not that ye are the temple of God, and that the Spirit of God dwelleth in you?" (1 Corinthians 3:16, KJV).

He is there but His presence may be latent. That's why you may not experience power or miracles although you are a child of God.

My "Latent Daughter"

When my wife became pregnant with my first daughter, Phoebe, I was both anxious and excited as I waited for her birth. She was present in my wife's womb but latent in my wife's womb and latent to me. I could not see, hear, smell, or even touch her, but yet still she was present.

When you become born again the Holy Ghost is present in your life but His power may not be manifest to your senses. Paul said to the new believers in the Church of Corinth, "Know ye not that ye are the temple of God, and that the Spirit of God dwelleth in you?" (1 Corinthians 3:16, KJV).

In other words they had all experienced "the presence of God." They were born again and the Holy Ghost was dwelling or living in them.

How I Came to Experience the Latent Presence

I became born again when I was eighteen years old. At that time my pastor, Bishop Dag Heward-Mills, was dating my sister and had come to visit her at home. One morning he called me aside and began to talk to me about becoming born again. I decided to give my life to Jesus, and on that day the Holy Ghost came to live in my heart.

From that day I started leading a holy life but I wondered if Christianity was all about not sinning. I was hungry to know the power of God but the Christian life seemed to be mundane. I went to church on Sundays, did what I had to do during the week, and the cycle seemed to repeat itself. Could there be more?

I knew the latent presence of God but not the manifest presence of God. I had never witnessed the power of God in any shape or fashion.

The Manifest Presence of the Holy Ghost

He Lives with You

The word "with" implies something external and visible. This seems to refer to the manifest presence of God. To be manifest means to be visible to the natural senses. When something is manifest you can see, hear, taste, smell, or touch it. When someone is with you, you can literally see him.

When the power of God became manifest in the life of Jesus He was described in this way, "how God anointed Jesus of Nazareth with the Holy Spirit and power, and how he went around doing good and healing all who were under the power of the devil, because God was with him" (Acts 10:38).

The presence of the Holy Ghost was manifested because the people could see cripples walking and the sick healed.

The Birth of My Daughter

I have four children, and I remember clearly when my first daughter Pheobe was born. It was a Sunday evening on the fifth of November. It was a joyous moment. She had been living or dwelling in my wife's womb for nine months, but on that day she became manifest to me. There she was, lying by her mother. I could see, touch, hear, and smell her. Now she is older and of great help in many ways. Just yesterday I was talking to her and she was telling me about different dishes she had cooked.

Our Helper

When you experience the manifest presence of the Holy Ghost, you will experience Him as a helper. You will experience Him as a helper because He will not just be *in* you; He will also be *with* you, like Phoebe is with me and of great help to me.

Look at how Jesus referred to Him: "But the Comforter, which is the Holy Ghost, whom the Father will send in my name, he shall teach you all things, and bring all things to your remembrance, whatsoever I have said unto you" (John 14:26, KJV).

The word comforter is the Greek word Parakletos. The original meaning of that word is someone who has been summed to aid, help, or assist another person.

Jesus and the Manifest Presence of the Holy Ghost

When Jesus came to the earth there was nothing about Him that suggested He was the Son of God till the Holy Spirit manifested Himself through Him at the marriage in Cana of Galilee. In that story Jesus turned water into wine at a wedding because the wine had run out.

"Jesus saith unto them, Fill the waterpots with water. And they filled them up to the brim. And he saith unto them, Draw out now, and bear unto the governor of the feast. And they bare it. When the ruler of the feast had tasted the water that was made wine, and knew not whence it was: (but the servants which drew the water knew;) the governor of the feast called the bridegroom, And saith unto him, Every man at the beginning doth set forth good wine; and when men have well drunk, then that which is worse: but thou hast kept the good wine until now. This beginning of miracles did Jesus in Cana of Galilee, and manifested forth his glory; and his disciples believed on him" (John 2:7-11, KJV).

Jesus "manifested forth His glory." That is the manifest presence of God. The disciples could see, smell, touch, and taste the wine.

Many people know the Lord but not many have experienced the manifest presence of God. They have not experienced the power of God through their senses.

A Testimony About the Manifest Presence of God

I remember once praying for a woman who owed about $100,000 on her mortgage. After some time her house was put up for sale. She came to see me with tears streaming down her face. She asked me to pray with her for a miraculous intervention. She had no alternative. After we prayed a perfect stranger paid the mortgage off within two days. The miraculous part was it was for free. Praise be to Jesus! This is an example of the manifest presence of God in someone's finances.

How do you move from the presence of God to the manifest presence of God? How can you also begin to witness the power of God?

CHAPTER 3

YOU MUST BE ABLE TO IDENTIFY HIM

Identification Means to Know Who Someone Is

TO EXPERIENCE the manifest presence of the Holy Ghost, you must be able to identify Him.

One day I asked a well-connected friend of mine to pick up another friend of mine, Michael, at the airport and give him a VIP experience. I gave him his picture so he could identify him at the gate. But he couldn't identify him till every single passenger had disembarked.

In the picture my friend was in spectacles, so he was looking for a man in spectacles. Unfortunately for him he was wearing contact lenses on that day so he couldn't be identified or helped. The Holy Ghost can only help you when you can identify Him.

Identifying Him Is Crucial

You cannot recognize or relate to someone you cannot identify. That's why this key is so important. The inability to recognize the Holy Ghost will lead to the inability to receive from Him. Jesus recognized this difficulty when He said, "And I will ask the Father, and he will give you another advocate to help you and be with you forever—the Spirit of truth. The world cannot accept him, because it neither sees him nor knows him. But you know him, for he lives with you and will be in you" (John 14:17).

CHAPTER 4

RELATE TO THE HOLY GHOST BY ONE OF HIS FORMS

TO IDENTIFY the Holy Ghost you must choose one of His forms that you can relate to.

The Incredible Hulk

The Incredible Hulk is one of the fictional Marvel superheroes. In the natural the Hulk is known as Bruce Banner, a weak, reserved, and withdrawn scientist. As an ordinary man he is very easy to relate to. When he gets angry he transforms into this huge, green, fierce, strong superhero who is very difficult to relate to. His mere sight will send you running.

You can choose to relate to Bruce Banner or the Hulk because they represent two different forms of the same person, but it easier to relate to Bruce Banner, who is a man. It therefore is better to choose Bruce Banner to relate to. In the same way, you must choose a form of the Holy Spirit that you can relate to.

My Difficulty in Identifying the Holy Ghost

One of my difficulties in relating to the Holy Spirit was because of how I imagined Him. I saw Him as a cloud or shadow that seemed to float around. This image was taken from the creation account.

He is introduced as a mysterious cloud or shadow that eerily moved over a dark wasteland. Looks more to me like a scene from a science fiction movie. I can imagine the sound of a mysterious wind blowing on a misty surface. This is the description: "In the beginning God created the heavens and the earth. Now the earth was formless and empty, darkness was over the surface of the deep, and the Spirit of God was hovering over the waters" (Genesis 1:1-2). Who can relate to a cloud that hovers and moves around? Sounds very spooky to me.

Added to this difficulty was how the Holy Ghost manifested as a wind and tongues of fire on the day of Pentecost. Who can befriend a wind or a fire? Will it not burn you? This mental image of mine was also drawn from what happened on the day of Pentecost: "And when the day of Pentecost was fully come, they were all with one accord in one place. And suddenly there came a sound from heaven as of a rushing mighty wind, and it filled all the house where they were sitting. And there appeared unto them cloven tongues like as of fire, and it sat upon each of them. And they were all filled with the Holy Ghost, and began to speak with other tongues, as the Spirit gave them utterance" (Acts 2:1-4, KJV).

Depending on which form of the Holy Ghost you choose, He can be a person with a definite form, or a shapeless spirit. The best way to identify Him is to identify Him as the ghost of Jesus.

CHAPTER 5

THE HOLY GHOST IS THE GHOST OF JESUS

TO IDENTIFY the Holy Ghost you must identify Him as the Ghost of Jesus.

Identification Is Key

Some years back I went on a three-day retreat with the sole aim of knowing the Holy Ghost in a tangible way. On the third day something dramatic happened that radically changed my relationship with the Holy Ghost.

Around 3 a.m. I was sitting in my chair, praying and discouraged because I thought I wasn't making any progress. Suddenly I audibly heard someone calling my name from the direction of the kitchen, "Kakra, Kakra, Kakra"; three times. I excitedly jumped to my feet and shouted, "Holy Ghost!" I knew without a shadow of doubt that the Holy Ghost was calling me. I had just experienced the manifest presence of God.

He asked me, "Do you know who I am?" I answered, "Who are you?" He responded, "I am the Ghost of Jesus." That was when everything fell into place for me. It was a very great revelation. Finally I could identify and put a form to Him. He was the Ghost of Jesus.

Understanding the Concept of a Ghost

It was easy for me to understand the concept of a ghost. When I was about twelve years old my grandmum passed away. Some nights I would wake up shivering with fright if I heard any noise. I was afraid her ghost had come to the house. A ghost is a spirit without a body.

I once watched a movie called *Ghost*. In the movie the ghost of a murdered man returned in an invisible form to haunt those who had killed him. I could relate to the concept of a ghost.

Jesus at the Point of Death

Let's examine what happened to Jesus when He was at the point of death. "Jesus, when he had cried again with a loud voice, yielded up the ghost. And, behold, the veil of the temple was rent in twain from the top to the bottom; and the earth did quake, and the rocks rent; And the graves were opened; and many bodies of the saints which slept arose, And came out of the graves after his resurrection, and went into the holy city, and appeared unto many" (Matthew 27:50-53, KJV).

When Jesus died His Spirit separated from His body. He "yielded up the ghost." His Spirit was then referred to as "the Ghost." His Ghost went to the cemetery and conducted a miracle service. He raised many dead people from the grave. "And the graves were opened; and many bodies of the saints which slept arose." This was to announce the manifest presence of the Holy Ghost. The Holy Ghost is the Ghost of Jesus.

Putting Form to the Holy Spirit

When you see Him as the Ghost of Jesus you can put form to Him. This is because the ghost of a person looks exactly like the physical image of the person. In my supernatural encounter with the Holy Ghost, He said to me, "I look just like Jesus because the ghost of a man looks just like the man."

My Auntie

When I was a kid an auntie of mine died. Unfortunately for me I mistook my dead auntie for for another auntie who was alive. A week after her death I was home alone when I heard someone ringing the bell. When I opened the door, lo and behold this "supposedly dead" auntie of mine was standing there. I couldn't believe my very eyes! My knees wobbled, my eyes dilated, the skin of my flesh stood up, and I run away from the "ghost." Later I got to know my mistake.

I believe one of the forms of the Holy Ghost is the form of Jesus in His human body. This is because the ghost of a person looks like the person.

The Ghost of a Person Looks Like Them

In the story of Lazarus and the rich man, there was a rich man who used to feed a certain poor man called Lazarus with leftovers from his house. One day they both died and they were both buried. Lazarus went to paradise and the rich man went to hell, "And in hell he lift up his eyes, being in torments, and seeth Abraham afar off, and Lazarus in his bosom" (Luke 16:23, KJV).

The rich man was able to identify Lazarus in paradise. It couldn't have been the physical body of Lazarus because he had been buried. He saw his ghost or spirit and he looked exactly like his physical form.

In another example, Jesus separated Himself from His disciples to spend time in prayer, "And in the fourth watch of the night Jesus went unto them, walking on the sea. And when the disciples saw him walking on the sea, they were troubled, saying, It is a spirit; and they cried out for fear" (Matthew 14:25-26, KJV). His disciples thought it was His spirit because His spirit looked like His physical form.

Once you can conceive in your mind that the Holy Spirit is the Ghost of Jesus, He will become very easy to relate to because He will have a form.

Faith and Boldness When I Preach

When I rise up to preach I am full of faith and boldness. This is because mentally I put form to the Holy Ghost and imagine Him as a real invisible person standing by me. As I walk to the pulpit I believe the Ghost of Jesus is walking with me. I can imagine Him, walking by me, sitting with me, and preaching with me.

In the pulpit I try to be His interpreter. A preacher is supposed to be the interpreter of Jesus. Jesus was the interpreter of the Father. This is what He said about Himself, "Don't you believe that I am in the Father, and that the

Father is in me? The words I say to you I do not speak on my own authority. Rather, it is the Father, living in me, who is doing his work" (John 14:10).

When you think like that you will have faith and be relaxed because you know that God is with you. No wonder the apostles performed many miracles, "Then the disciples went out and preached everywhere, and the Lord worked with them and confirmed his word by the signs that accompanied it" (Mark 16:20).

Obviously Mark, who wrote this piece, saw the Holy Ghost as the Ghost of Jesus because he referred to Him as the Lord. He said, "The Lord worked with them"—not a fire or a wind—but the Lord. Who is this Lord? "Now the Lord is that Spirit" (2 Corinthians 3:17). The Ghost of the Lord Jesus worked with the disciples.

The Ghost of Jesus is ready to accomplish His will through you. All you need to do is to cooperate with Him.

The Healing of the Paralyzed Woman

I once went to preach in a little town where I witnessed a great miracle. At the end of the last evening session I was about to close when the Holy Ghost said to me, "Do you want to experience a miracle?" I said, "Yes, Lord." He said, "Do you see that woman lying in front of the stage?" I said, "Yes, Lord." That particular woman had been lying there since I started preaching. He said to me, "Announce to the church that she will be healed in the next five minutes."

I protested, "Lord, what about if she is not healed? I will be embarrassed." After a little mental tussle I decided to step out in faith. I said to the congregation, "This woman lying here is about to be healed in the next five minutes."

I continued, "Who brought this woman here?" A family of about five walked up to me. They told me what had happened to her. She had fallen from a building and as a result had become paralyzed. She couldn't even stand. I was stunned. I didn't know it was such a serious case before I made that bold proclamation. My throat became dry and I was trapped by my own words.

The Holy Spirit said to me, "Ask them to raise her up and prop her on all sides so she can stand." I mustered faith and said it and the family obeyed. After I said, "Holy Ghost, what next?" He said, "Now ask them to stop supporting her and back away." I protested, "What about if she falls and her head hits the floor?" I was sweating on the inside but appeared cool on the outside. He said, "Just do it."

I said to them, "All of you leave her and back away." They left and miraculously she was standing on her feet, unaided but swaying gently from side to side like she was about to fall. Then He said, "Take her hand and pull her a little bit closer to you." When I did so she took a faltering, tottering step. I pulled again and she took another step. I noticed her gait was getting firmer and firmer as I pulled. After about ten she steps she broke free and started running; the power of God hit her. All hell broke loose with excitement! The Holy Ghost had manifested Himself and glorified the name of Jesus.

One thing that helped my faith was my ability to put form to Him. To me the Ghost of Jesus was standing by me and instructing me. I was not responsible for the miracle—He was.

Freedom from Responsibility of Healing

If you can conceive of the Holy Spirit as the Ghost of Jesus, it will free you from the responsibility of healing.

Sometimes I take my kids out to eat. They order whatever they want to eat without thinking about it although they have no money in their pockets. They order in faith because they know they are not responsible for the payment. They know I am present with them and I will pay the bill.

If you can have faith that the Ghost of Jesus is with you, you can have the boldness and faith to "order healing" because you know He will pay the bill, "But my God shall supply all your need according to his riches in glory by Christ Jesus" (Philippians 4:19, KJV).

I am glad He is in charge of the supply of healing, miracles, finances, marriage, anointing, etc.

CHAPTER 6

SEE THE HOLY GHOST AS JESUS

TO IDENTIFY the Holy Ghost, you must see Him as the same Jesus who used to walk on the earth without His body.

Jesus Is Still on the Earth

If you were to learn that Jesus had returned to the earth I am sure that you would have faith that He could heal you of any sickness. I have good news for you. He never left. His Ghost is still with us, "Now the Lord is that Spirit" (2 Corinthians 3:17, KJV).

That's why I love these words from the song, "There Is a Redeemer," by Keith Green: "Thank you, O my Father, for giving us Your Son and leaving Your Spirit till the work on earth is done."

Sometimes people tell me they have seen me in their dreams, praying for them. I believe the person they see is not me but my spirit, who looks just like me. I have been seen in far-off places like China praying for people, meanwhile physically I will be at home with my wife.

A Testimony

This is a testimony someone sent to me. It's an example of what I am talking about.

Dear Kakra,

> I saw you preaching on Facebook and towards the end of the service you stopped and prophesied that someone with a chronic disease is being healed.

I had been suffering from a terrible migraine for the past ten years.

After your prayer I dreamt I was vomiting tumors with lots of blood. I was taken to the hospital and at the car park you saw me and quickly came to pray for me. You breathed three times into each ear. Immediately, the tumors vanished from my ear. As you kept praying someone came with a stretched arm saying, "Come home to Glory," but you rebuked the person and said, "She is going nowhere. She belongs to Jesus."

When I woke up my ears had become very clear and I have been healed of this terrible migraine.

God be praised! I believe this person saw my spirit man, who looks just like me.

How Is That Possible?

One thing you must understand is that the principles of the spirit realm are very different from the natural realm. That's why you must not compare the two. It's like trying to compare the computing world to the natural world. They are different realms.

In the Spirit it is possible to be in two places at the same time, but this is not possible in the natural. In Paul's letter to the Church of Corinth he told them that his spirit would be present with them when they met to pray although physically he was in another location. He said, "So when you are assembled and I am with you in spirit, and the power of our Lord Jesus is present…" (1 Corinthians 5:4).

Jesus Was Present in Two Places

When Jesus ascended up to heaven He became present in two places: heaven and earth. Look at what happened after His resurrection, "After the Lord Jesus had spoken to them, he was taken up into heaven and he sat at the right hand of God. Then the disciples went out and preached everywhere, and the Lord worked with them and confirmed his word by the signs that accompanied it" (Mark 16:19-20).

I want you to notice, the same Lord who ascended up to heaven to sit on the right hand of God was also on the earth working with the disciples, "the Lord worked with them." Who is this Lord referred to here who was working with the disciples on the earth? "Now the Lord is the Spirit, and where the Spirit of the Lord is, there is freedom" (2 Corinthians 3:17). The Lord referred to here is the Spirit, who is also known as the Holy Ghost.

Some people think that Jesus is only seated on the right hand of God so He cannot be present on the earth. Because He is a spirit He can be present in multiple locations.

Now that you can identify Him, the next question is, "Why is it so important to know?"

CHAPTER 7

WHY IS IT IMPORTANT TO KNOW THE HOLY GHOST?

Who You Know Is More Important Than What You Know

ONE DAY SOMEONE I knew desperately wanted a job. She had been told there was no vacancy where she was seeking for employment. When she told me, I told her the manager was a good friend of mine so I would speak to him. When I called him he decided to hire this girl primarily because of who she knew but not what she knew.

Life is like that. At a certain point we all have the same skills, experience, etc. What will propel you to the next level will be dependent on who you know, not what you know.

Who you know is more important than what you know. Because of this people make great efforts to be connected to politicians, people of power, influencers, etc.

The most important person to know is the Holy Spirit. Let me give you one good reason why this is so important.

God is the creator and owner of the universe, "The earth is the LORD's, and everything in it, the world, and all who live in it" (Psalm 24:1, KJV). To receive anything from Him you must understand that He has handed over that responsibility to the Holy Ghost.

CHAPTER 8

THE HOLY GHOST IS THE CUSTODIAN

The Custodian

THE HOLY GHOST is the custodian of all that God has for you. A custodian is someone who is entrusted to keep something valuable. The Holy Ghost has in His custody your peace, salvation, finances, marital partner, your ministry, and everything on this earth.

Recently I went to cash some money at the bank. I handed over my signed cheque to the bank teller. After some checks and administrative procedures the teller handed over the cash to me. Now I was physically in possession of the money.

This is a little parable. Let's assume that the bank is God, who owns all the resources of the universe. The signature on the cheque is the name of Jesus, that authorizes the release of the money; and the teller is the Holy Spirit, who gave me the money.

In this example each person or member of the Godhead is important, with each playing a critical and unique role. Ultimately I had to receive the money from the teller, "the Holy Ghost."

When God wants to give you something He will give it to the Holy Ghost to give it to you. He is the giver of all that God has for you: your marriage, anointing, ministry, wisdom, power, finances, etc.

When This Arrangement Was Instituted

This arrangement was instituted after the resurrection of Christ. It seems to me throughout human history a particular member of the Trinity has interacted with man. From creation to the birth of Christ, God the Father interacted directly with man. From the time of Jesus to His death, it was the Son, Jesus. After the death and resurrection of Christ Jesus it is now the turn of the Holy Ghost. After the resurrection of Christ the Holy Ghost became the channel through which we receive what God has for us.

Instructions Are Given by the Holy Spirit

After His resurrection Jesus gave instructions indirectly through the Holy Spirit. This is how this arrangement is presented in the book of Acts, "The former treatise have I made, O Theophilus, of all that Jesus began both to do and teach, Until the day in which he was taken up, after that he through the Holy Ghost had given commandments unto the apostles whom he had chosen" (Acts 1:1-2, KJV).

I want you to notice, Jesus started giving commands through the Holy Ghost, not directly to the disciples, as He used to do when He was alive. Why is that so? Because the arrangement had changed.

Power Is Given by the Holy Spirit

Also power has to be received from Him. This suggests He is the custodian of it, "But ye shall receive power, after that the Holy Ghost is come upon you" (Acts 1:8, KJV).

To have access to anything that God has for you, you have to go through Him, "For through him we both have access by one Spirit unto the Father" (Ephesians 2:18, KJV). "The person without the Spirit does not accept the things that come from the Spirit of God but considers them foolishness, and cannot understand them because they are discerned only through the Spirit" (1 Corinthians 2:14).

CHAPTER 9

THE MARRIAGE OF ISAAC AND SARAH

The Holy Spirit Is the Custodian of God's Blessings

THE MARRIAGE OF Isaac and Sarah can be viewed as a parable that shows us the role of the Holy Spirit as the custodian of God's blessings. A parable is a story with a hidden meaning. Most of the Old Testament stories are parables that talk about Jesus. Jesus Himself taught His disciples this principle, "And beginning with Moses and all the Prophets, he explained to them what was said in all the Scriptures concerning himself" (Luke 24:27).

"Moses" means the five Old Testament books written by Moses: Genesis to Deuteronomy. The "prophets" mean the Old Testament prophetic books written by prophets like Isaiah and Jeremiah. Jesus said all those books are parables concerning Him.

In this story Abraham sent his servant to look for a wife for his son, Isaac. This can also be viewed as a parable about the marriage of Christ to His Bride, the Church. Let's look at some portions of the story, "Abraham was now very old, and the LORD had blessed him in every way. He said to the senior servant in his household, the one in charge of all that he had, 'Put your hand under my thigh. I want you to swear by the LORD, the God of heaven and the God of earth, that you will not get a wife for my son from the daughters of the Canaanites, among whom I am living, but will go to my country and my own relatives and get a wife for my son Isaac' " (Genesis 24:1-4).

When the servant arrived in the land he prayed that God would bless him and make his mission successful, "Then he prayed, 'Lord, God of my master Abraham, make me successful today, and show kindness to my master Abraham. See, I am standing beside this spring, and the daughters of the townspeople are coming out to draw water. May it be that when I say to a young woman, "Please let down your jar that I may have a drink," and she says, "Drink, and I'll water your camels too"—let her be the one you have chosen for your servant Isaac. By this I will know that you have shown kindness to my master'" (Genesis 24:12-14).

The servant chose Rebekah and went to seek her hand from her parents. He told them: "The Lord has blessed my master abundantly, and he has become wealthy. He has given him sheep and cattle, silver and gold, male and female servants, and camels and donkeys. My master's wife Sarah has borne him a son in her old age, and he has given him everything he owns" (Genesis 24:35-36).

The servant gave gifts to Rebekah and her family, "Then the servant brought out gold and silver jewelry and articles of clothing and gave them to Rebekah; he also gave costly gifts to her brother and to her mother" (Genesis 24:53). "So they called Rebekah and asked her, 'Will you go with this man?' 'I will go,' she said" (Genesis 24:58). The servant returned with Rebekah to an unknown land to marry an unknown person.

The Holy Ghost As a Custodian Explained

This parable explains the role of the Holy Ghost as a custodian. The characters in the story represent the following.

- Abraham is symbolic of God, the Father.
- Isaac, his son, is symbolic of Jesus, the Son of God.
- The servant is the Holy Ghost, who carries out the wishes of the Father and the Son.
- Rebekah represents you and me; the Bride of Christ, or the Church.

I want us to look at some examples of some of the valuable things He has in His custody.

The Holy Ghost Is the Custodian of Revelation

Only the Servant Could Reveal the Knowledge about Abraham and Isaac

Rebekah had no knowledge about Isaac or Abraham. She had to rely solely on the servant. Only the Holy Ghost can grant you knowledge and revelation about God. Sometimes I can know things about people and situations through the revelation of the Holy Ghost.

I Had a Revelation About a Certain Pastor

A pastor once came to see me for prayer because his church was not growing. The Holy Ghost revealed to me the reason. The pastor had an affair with another pastor's wife when he went to minister in their church. He confirmed it was true, and I asked him to repent and change his ways.

One Day Jesus Asked His Disciples About His Identity

"They replied, 'Some say John the Baptist; others say Elijah; and still others, Jeremiah or one of the prophets.' 'But what about you?' he asked. 'Who do you say I am?' Simon Peter answered, 'You are the Messiah, the Son of the living God.' Jesus replied, 'Blessed are you, Simon son of Jonah, for this was not revealed to you by flesh and blood, but by my Father in heaven' " (Matthew 16:14-17).

Whatever Rebekah knew about the Father and the Son was based on what the servant, the Holy Ghost, revealed to her.

He Is the Custodian of the Gifts and Provision of God

The Gifts the Servant Gave Rebekah Represent the Gifts of God

Without the servant, the Holy Ghost, you cannot receive the gifts of God, either tangible or intangible.

I recently prayed for a depressed, divorced woman and prophesied that God had healed her and He was going to give her a new husband. Within a year she met a wonderful man and got married. She is happily married now. "Houses and wealth are inherited from parents, but a prudent wife is from the LORD" (Proverbs 19:14).

Truly the Holy Ghost is the channel through which God gives gifts to His children. These gifts may be spiritual things like the anointing or a tangible thing like a job. "He who did not spare his own Son, but gave him up for us all—how will he not also, along with him, graciously give us all things?" (Romans 8:32).

He Is the Custodian of "Heaven"

Abraham and Isaac lived in a different town and it was the servant who brought Rebekah to where Isaac lived to be wedded. One day the Holy Ghost will resurrect all Christians, and they will marry the Bridegroom, Christ. "And if the Spirit of him who raised Jesus from the dead is living in you, he who raised Christ from the dead will also give life to your mortal bodies because of his Spirit who lives in you" (Romans 8:11).

After resurrection we will be transported to heaven to marry the Bridegroom, Christ. This marriage made in heaven will be made possible by the servant, the Holy Ghost. This prophecy encapsulates this: "Let us rejoice and be glad and give him glory! For the wedding of the Lamb has come, and his bride has made herself ready" (Revelation 19:7).

CHAPTER 10

HE IS THE CUSTODIAN OF GOD'S POWER

WHEN I WAS A KID there was an ice cream man who sold ice cream in our school. I used to anxiously look through the window at break time to see if I could see his bike. His presence meant ice cream was available.

I didn't look for the ice cream; I only looked for the man, since he was the custodian of the ice cream. The Holy Ghost is the custodian of the power of God. That's why Jesus said, "But ye shall receive power, after that the Holy Ghost is come upon you: and ye shall be witnesses unto me both in Jerusalem, and in all Judaea, and in Samaria, and unto the uttermost part of the earth" (Acts 1:8, KJV).

Are you looking for power? Don't look for power; look for the Holy Ghost. When the Holy Ghost comes you will receive power. Power is given by the Holy Ghost. Instead of praying for power, pray that you may know the Holy Ghost. That's why Paul said, "That I may know him, and the power of his resurrection" (Philippians 3:10, KJV).

A Woman Healed of Cancer

One day I was in a meeting when a woman suffering from cancer was wheeled into the meeting. Her skin was becoming blackish and she looked gaunt and pale. According to her a wind blew across the room when I started praying. A force blew her off the wheelchair and unto the ground. She started screaming. After that encounter the cancer vanished and she was healed completely. Praise be to God! She received power when the Holy Ghost manifested Himself. This concept is seen in the healing of Aeneas.

The Healing of Aeneas

Peter travelled to a city called Lydda, "And there he found a certain man named Aeneas, which had kept his bed eight years, and was sick of the palsy. And Peter said unto him, Aeneas, Jesus Christ maketh thee whole: arise, and make thy bed. And he arose immediately" (Acts 9:33-34, KJV).

I can almost imagine the scene. Peter walks into this sick disciple's bedroom. Suddenly his eyes are open in the Spirit realm and he sees Jesus standing by the bed of the sick man. No one sees him but him. This is because he is seeing the Ghost of Jesus, the Holy Ghost, who looks exactly like Him. He refers to the Holy Ghost who is resident on earth as Jesus Christ. He says, "Aeneas, Jesus Christ makes you whole." Immediately power was released by the Holy Ghost and the man was healed. It also makes me remember the healing of a Muslim with a mental problem.

A Muslim Healed of a Mental Problem

Sometime back I went to preach in a town that was predominantly Muslim. During the second night a Muslim came to share a testimony with me. He said he came for the service because he needed healing for his son who had a mental problem. After I finished preaching they went back home with his son still in the same condition.

But something happened that night. His son was asleep when he felt someone rousing him from sleep. When he looked he saw a man dressed in a glowing white robe. The man pulled something out of the boy's head and walked away. He was healed instantly of schizophrenia.

I believe he saw the Ghost of Jesus and He healed him. The family became Christians because of this. Praise be to God!

This brings to my mind a healing Scripture. James taught the Church how to obtain healing in times of sickness. He started with a question, "Is any sick among you? let him call for the elders of the church; and let them pray over him, anointing him with oil in the name of the Lord: And the prayer of faith shall save the sick, and the Lord shall raise him up; and if he have committed sins, they shall be forgiven him" (James 5:14-15).

James said that after praying over the sick person in faith with the anointing of oil, the Lord Jesus will come into the room and heal the man: "The Lord shall raise him up." Who is this Lord? I believe he is referring to the Ghost of Jesus. Remember that, "Now the Lord is that Spirit: and where the Spirit of the Lord is, there is liberty" (2 Corinthians 3:17, KJV).

CHAPTER 11

HE IS THE CUSTODIAN OF SPIRITUAL AND MINISTRY GIFTS

The Servant Gave Gifts to Rebekah

THE GIFTS THE SERVANT gave to Rebekah can symbolize ministry and spiritual gifts. Ministry gifts are for serving the body of Christ or the Church, and spiritual gifts are for every believer, "Then the servant brought out gold and silver jewelry and articles of clothing and gave them to Rebekah; he also gave costly gifts to her brother and to her mother" (Genesis 24:53).

My First Encounter with Jesus

When I was nineteen years old, Jesus appeared to me for the first time. I woke up early in the morning to pray on top of our roof, which was a concrete slab and also served as a large open balcony. We lived about two hundred meters from the sea, and I could feel the sea breeze licking my face that early morning. It was 3 a.m.

After praying for a while I felt this heavy presence begin to mount on the roof. I could sense something was coming, so I ran away. When I got to the door I couldn't open it because my hand was not responding to the command of my brain. It was rebelling against my will.

Suddenly the whole world lit up and I saw Jesus descending from the clouds. I shook with fear and trembled. I fell down on my face and pleaded for my life.

It was at that point that I received the call of God to enter the ministry. Someone asked me what He looked like.

He had the silhouette of a man but He seemed to be made out of light. It was then I understood that God is truly light.

From that time I made a decision to be a full-time minister. It was the Holy Ghost who made it possible for me to see all this and receive the ministry of a prophet. The natural senses cannot comprehend it.

Spiritual Gifts Are Given by Him

After the experience of seeing Jesus I was praying some days later when I fell to the ground because of the presence of the Holy Ghost. The Lord told me that He had given me the gift of discerning of spirits, "All these are the work of one and the same Spirit, and he distributes them to each one, just as he determines" (1 Corinthians 12:11).

Since I received this gift I have seen Jesus, angels, demons, and all types of spirits. Many have been delivered because of this gift. You cannot operate in spiritual gifts except the Holy Ghost gives it you.

"Now to each one the manifestation of the Spirit is given for the common good. To one there is given through the Spirit a message of wisdom, to another a message of knowledge by means of the same Spirit, to another faith by the same Spirit, to another gifts of healing by that one Spirit, to another miraculous powers, to another prophecy, to another distinguishing between spirits, to another speaking in different kinds of tongues, and to still another the interpretation of tongues. All these are the work of one and the same Spirit, and he distributes them to each one, just as he determines" (1 Corinthians 12:7-11).

A Remarkable Example of the Gift of Healing

A pastor once came to see me concerning his dad, who had been bedridden for eight years. I couldn't physically go with him. Sometimes I pray over a bottle of anointing oil, so I asked him to anoint his dad with the oil I had anointed. When he got home he did exactly that. A few minutes after he had some visitors, so he briefly went out to attend to them.

When he went back he saw a huge snake lying by his dad. He couldn't believe his eyes. The power of the gift of healing had physically exposed the evil spirit behind his dad's sickness. In case you don't know, the devil can manifest physically. Paul warned that in the last days we would have such occurrences.

Paul's Warning in the Last Days

Paul said, "But mark this: There will be terrible times in the last days" (2 Timothy 3:1). Then he gave an example, "Just as Jannes and Jambres opposed Moses, so also these teachers oppose the truth. They are men of depraved minds, who, as far as the faith is concerned, are rejected" (2 Timothy 3:8). Jannes and Jambres were the two magicians who turned rods into snakes when they came into confrontation with Moses.

The pastor who's dad was sick went out and called a friend. They came in with clubs and killed the snake. The sick man immediately rose from his sickbed completely healed. Praise be to Jesus! The gift of healing, which is given by the Holy Ghost, was working.

CHAPTER 12

HE IS THE CUSTODIAN OF GOD'S FINANCES

Rebekah Receives Riches

THE SERVANT GAVE Rebekah riches. These riches also reflected on her family members, "Then the servant brought out gold and silver jewelry and articles of clothing and gave them to Rebekah; he also gave costly gifts to her brother and to her mother" (Genesis 24:53).

The Holy Ghost can influence men and situations and bless you financially. God told Israel, "But remember the LORD your God, for it is he who gives you the ability to produce wealth, and so confirms his covenant, which he swore to your ancestors, as it is today" (Deuteronomy 8:18).

My Experience in Tamale

There is a town in Ghana called Tamale and I once went to preach in that town. After the service I was in my room when I fell into a trance. I walked into this expensive hotel with golden floors. The staff started dragging me out because they said the hotel was for very rich people and I did not qualify to be there since I didn't have a lot of money.

As the scuffle continued I heard someone say, "Leave him alone." When I turned I saw Jesus sitting at the corner of the lobby and He seemed to be sipping something. He asked me what the problem was. When I told Him, He said, "Don't worry." He was wearing a beautiful white robe and He removed it and put it on me.

He said, "From today there is nothing you need that you cannot afford." He continued, "To prove to you that this vision is true, I am going to send a total stranger to you. He will give you a set of instructions. Obey them and there will be a financial miracle to prove this vision is true." Then the vision ended. Not long after the stranger visited me.

A Visit from a Stranger

I was in my office when I was told a stranger was looking for me. After he was ushered into my office the stranger told me he had come with the sole purpose to bless me financially. Then I remembered the words of Jesus.

The stranger told me there was only one condition: I had to give him some money first. I don't remember the exact amount but it was anything between five to then thousand dollars. At that time that money was very huge. I told him to return after a couple of days for the money.

Now I was in a quandary. Do I believe God with bold faith, or hand over my money to a stranger? I decided to take a risky step of faith. I got the money and gave it to him. He told me he would be back and disappeared with my money.

A tear rolled down my eye. After some days he returned and he blessed me tremendously with a great financial blessing which would have taken me more than ten years to obtain. I am even afraid to mention it. The Holy Ghost can influence people and He uses events to bless you.

The Apostles and the Church Blessed Financially

The apostles and the Church were blessed financially by the Holy Spirit. The apostles came under great persecution. They were warned not to preach in the name of Jesus. Because of this a period of prayer was declared.

"After they prayed, the place where they were meeting was shaken. And they were all filled with the Holy Spirit and spoke the word of God boldly. All the believers were one in heart and mind. No one claimed that any of their possessions was their own, but they shared everything they had. With great power the apostles continued to testify to the resurrection of the Lord Jesus. And God's grace was so powerfully at work in them all that there were no needy persons among them. For from time to time those who owned land or houses sold them, brought the money from the sales and put it at the apostles' feet, and it was distributed to anyone who had need" (Acts 4:31-35).

People sold houses and land and brought the money to the apostles. Has anyone ever sold his house and given the money to you? It takes the power of the Holy Ghost to enjoy such grace. There was no poor person in the Church.

A Project with My Siblings

Sometime back some of my siblings and I embarked on a project. Two years before the inception of the project I had a vision from the Holy Ghost. He told me about it and told me God wanted to bless me through it. I put it on my "prophecy shelf" and waited for the time to be fulfilled.

Two years after the vision my brother Moses came to tell me about a project he had in mind. It was that same project, and immediately I knew that the Holy Ghost was ready to give me what God had showed me. We did the project, and it has been a great blessing to me. "And my God will meet all your needs according to the riches of his glory in Christ Jesus" (Philippians 4:19). These riches have already been provided in glory or eternity.

CHAPTER 13

HE IS THE CUSTODIAN OF SALVATION

Only the Holy Spirit Can Sanctify

ONLY THE SERVANT could bring Rebekah to Isaac. Only the Holy Spirit can bring you to Christ. Peter said we "have been chosen according to the foreknowledge of God the Father, through the sanctifying work of the Spirit, to be obedient to Jesus Christ and sprinkled with his blood" (1 Peter 1:2).

To sanctify means set apart. Only the Holy Ghost can pull you away from sin, the flesh, the world, the club, bad company, pride, pornography, sex, bitterness, etc., and cause you to be washed by the blood of the Lamb.

My Friend Larry

My friend Larry experienced one of the most dramatic conversions I have ever witnessed. He was pestering one of my Christian fellowship members with offers of love. The problem was, she was a committed Christian and he was not, so she had decided to distance herself from him, but he was in hot pursuit.

This young lady shared her dilemma with me and asked me what could be done about it. I told her, for his "punishment" we would pray that the Holy Ghost would convict him and make him a born-again Christian. It was around twelve midnight when we started praying for him.

I later got to know that around that same time Larry was walking alone on a dark, deserted road, smoking and going home. Suddenly he felt a strong conviction in his heart that he needed to surrender his life to Jesus. This freak conviction became so strong he started weeping like a baby. He went down on his knees and gave his life to Jesus. Larry married the young woman, and now is a fine minister of God.

The Holy Ghost is the giver of salvation. He convicts us of sin and comes to dwell in our hearts.

The Day of Pentecost

On the day of Pentecost the Holy Ghost saved many people, "When the day of Pentecost came, they were all together in one place. Suddenly a sound like the blowing of a violent wind came from heaven and filled the whole house where they were sitting. They saw what seemed to be tongues of fire that separated and came to rest on each of them. All of them were filled with the Holy Spirit and began to speak in other tongues as the Spirit enabled them" (Acts 2:1-4).

Peter preached a very powerful sermon, "When the people heard this, they were cut to the heart and said to Peter and the other apostles, 'Brothers, what shall we do?' Peter replied, 'Repent and be baptized, every one of you, in the name of Jesus Christ for the forgiveness of your sins. And you will receive the gift of the Holy Spirit. The promise is for you and your children and for all who are far off—for all whom the Lord our God will call' " (Acts 2:37-39). "Those who accepted his message were baptized, and about three thousand were added to their number that day" (Acts 2:41).

Without the Holy Ghost you cannot become a child of God because He alone can convict you of sin. This was summed up nicely by Jesus when He said, "When he comes, he will prove the world to be in the wrong about sin and righteousness and judgment" (John 16:8). "No one can come to me unless the Father who sent me draws them, and I will raise them up at the last day" (John 6:44).

Some Important Questions

At this point I want to ask you some questions. Are you saved? Do you know where your soul will spend eternity?

Have your sins been washed by the blood of Jesus? Do you know Him as your Savior? If you answered no to any of these questions and you want to know Jesus as your personal Lord and Savior, this is what you need to do.

First of all you need to repent of your sins. Secondly you have to believe that Jesus died for your sin and His blood washes away sin. Finally you have to invite Him to dwell in your heart.

Let's pray. Lord Jesus, I acknowledge that I am a sinner. I believe that You died for me and Your blood can wash away my sins. Come and dwell in my heart, Holy Ghost, and make me a child of God. Thank You for coming into my heart. In Jesus' name. Amen.

If you prayed this prayer with me, it means you are a now a child of God.

CHAPTER 14

YOU NEED AN INTRODUCTION

All My Good Friends Were Introduced to Me

I HAVE TWO CHILDHOOD friends, Armso and Charles, whom I have known for many years. I got to know Armso at the age of eight and Charles at the age of eleven. Till this day we are still very close friends. I remember the first time I was introduced to Armso. I was in class two at that time and one morning he joined our class as a new student. During break one of my friends, Selah, introduced him to me.

There was a picture of Jesus on one of our classroom walls. Armso pointed to it and said he was more handsome than Jesus. I started arguing with him that no one could be more handsome than Jesus, and from there our friendship began and it has developed over the years. Charles was introduced to my by my big brother, Sidney. To know the Holy Spirit you must first be introduced to Him.

Jesus Introduces the Holy Ghost

Jesus must introduce you to the Holy Ghost. That is why you must get to know Jesus, because He is the only one who can introduce you to the Holy Ghost.

Peter preached a powerful sermon to a great crowd on the the day of Pentecost, "Then Peter said unto them, Repent, and be baptized every one of you in the name of Jesus Christ for the remission of sins, and ye shall receive the gift of the Holy Ghost" (Acts 2:38, KJV). In summary, he said, to receive the Holy Ghost you must first be introduced by Jesus and then "you will receive the gift of the Holy Spirit."

The Holy Ghost will then come and dwell in you, "Know ye not that ye are the temple of God, and that the Spirit of God dwelleth in you?" (1 Corinthians 3:16, KJV). This will mark the beginning of your friendship with the Ghost of Jesus. That's when you become born again. Generally speaking, you become a citizen of the country where you were born. "The LORD will write in the register of the peoples: 'This one was born in Zion' " (Psalm 87:6).

God will register your name, give you a spiritual birth certificate, and it will be proof that you are a citizen.

CHAPTER 15

YOU MUST TALK TO HIM

The Importance of Prayer

YOU MUST TALK to the Holy Spirit to develop a relationship with Him. That's what makes prayer important.

The first time I saw my wife I was in my first year in college. I was standing in front of an all-male hall of residence when this white Mercedes pulled up. Out stepped this beautiful young lady. Immediately she caught my attention and I wondered who she was. I noticed a certain gentleman was waiting for her and she got out and chatted with this lucky fellow for a while. I had never seen her before but she left a mark on my mind. Later I got to learn from friends she was a medical student and we were in the same-year group.

Fortunately for me, my next-door neighbor, David, was an old friend from high school and also her mate. I asked him many questions about her and I got to know she was a very committed Christian as well.

This peaked my interest and my heart was stirred. The Holy Ghost said to me, "You will marry that girl." It's amazing how God can use our desires to guide us. Truly the heart of a man is the steering wheel of God. "The king's heart is in the hand of the LORD, as the rivers of water: he turneth it whithersoever he will" (Proverbs 21:1, KJV).

I began to plan my first move to get acquainted with her. I tried a blind date through a friend of mine, but it didn't work. But as providence would have it, one day I was having coffee with a mutual friend of ours, Naakai, when she came to join us. My moment had arrived. I said, "Lord, glorify your son and your son will also glorify You."

On that day she was introduced to me. From there we started talking. Every day. We sent notes and letters to each other and the more we talked the closer we became. Words can supply life to a relationship or choke it to death. "The tongue has the power of life and death, and those who love it will eat its fruit" (Proverbs 18:21). Someone told me, "I have been verbally abused by my husband for a long time and it has killed my love for him." Negative words produce the fruit of death.

Positive Words Give Life to a Relationship
When you look into the eyes of someone you love and say, "Honey, when I'm with you I feel like I'm back in my mother's womb and I feel I want to spend eternity with you," you will be supplying life to the relationship because words are what makes love grow.

A married woman told me she had spent so much time talking to someone she felt she was falling in love with the person. Are you being emotionally drawn to someone you should not be loving? Maybe a married person or a friend's lover? One way to deal with it is to choke the life out of it.

Cease communicating with the person and you will gradually asphyxiate it and choke it to death. That's what makes prayer important if you are to know the Holy Spirit and fall in love with Him.

When you pray you are holding a conversation with the Holy Spirit, and your relationship and love for Him will grow. I can spend hours in prayer and fellowship with the Holy Ghost.

Jesus' Friendship with the Holy Ghost
Jesus developed His friendship with the Holy Ghost through prayer. At the baptism of Jesus the Holy Ghost came upon Him as He was praying. Prayer is one of the things that attracts His presence. "When all the people were being baptized, Jesus was baptized too. And as he was praying, heaven was opened and the Holy Spirit descended on him in bodily form like a dove. And a voice came from

heaven: 'You are my Son, whom I love; with you I am well pleased' " (Luke 3:21-22).

Their relationship moved to a higher level when He spent forty days and nights praying. This time, "Jesus, full of the Holy Spirit, left the Jordan and was led by the Spirit into the wilderness" (Luke 4:1). "Jesus returned to Galilee in the power of the Spirit, and news about him spread through the whole countryside" (Luke 4:14).

Many of my encounters and revelations of the Holy Ghost have come through periods of prayer and fasting. The more I pray or chat with Him the more our relationship grows.

Talking is a two-way street. As we talk to God, He also talks back to us. Sometimes in revelations, visions, and dreams. Through this He also communicates with you and reveals Himself to you.

My Vision of the Grace of God

The Holy Ghost once gave me a vision of the grace of God. You can read about the grace of God in the Bible, but it's another thing to have a revelation about it. Revelation deepens your understanding of spiritual concepts.

In this vision I was in heaven and standing before the throne of God. There was a huge screen that was showing a movie of a very wicked man. He was a liar, a cheat, etc. As I stared at the screen I wondered who would be bold enough to do all this before the presence of God. Suddenly the man turned and I saw his face. Do you know who it was? It was me. Like Isaiah the prophet, I said, "Woe is me! for I am undone; because I am a man of unclean lips, and I dwell in the midst of a people of unclean lips: for mine eyes have seen the King, the Lord of hosts" (Isaiah 6:5, KJV).

Surprisingly the Lord said to the angels, "Promote this man." I was in utter shock and disbelief because I felt I deserved judgment. Then the Lord said to me, "You are standing before the throne of grace and here only mercy and grace is given."

There is a Scripture that says, "Let us therefore come boldly unto the throne of grace, that we may obtain mercy, and find grace to help in time of need" (Hebrews 4:16, KJV). It deepened my understanding about the grace of God.

That's what prayer can do. It can deepen your knowledge about God and grow your relationship with Him.

CHAPTER 16

YOU MUST KNOW HIM

TO DEVELOP YOUR relationship with the Holy Ghost, you must know Him.

Knowledge Is Key

Pastor Brian has been a friend of mine and my assistant pastor for many years. I got to know him in university. I used to be the leader of a prayer fellowship when I was in the university. After my undergraduate degree I took a gap year for practical training. It was at that time that he came to join our fellowship. Upon my return I learnt a great praise and worship leader had joined us from a certain church and his name was Brian.

Immediately I became suspicious of him because a friend of mine had earlier told me about a very good praise and worship leader from that same church who was a womanizer. I assumed it was Brian. I was therefore not happy with him at all but everyone seemed to think he was a good Christian and a spiritual person. I decided to observe him myself. Over time I got to know more about him and I became convinced he was a genuine person.

One day my friend who had told me about the womanizer came to visit me and I pointed out Brian to him. He laughed and told it was not Brian but another person. He highly recommended Brian. I didn't trust Brian because I knew very little about him.

Little children are usually told not to talk to strangers. This is because you cannot trust someone you don't know. Knowledge breeds transparency, which births trust. Trust is one of the foundations of all successful relationships. We tend to be skeptical towards people we don't know but be close and relaxed with people we know.

You Must Know Him to Trust Him

You cannot be close to or trust the Holy Ghost when you know very little about Him. One way to know Him is through the Scriptures. The Scriptures contain the knowledge of God. That's why you must read the Bible to know the Holy Spirit. Jesus said, "You study the Scriptures diligently because you think that in them you have eternal life. These are the very Scriptures that testify about me" (John 5:39).

Jesus' relationship with the Holy Ghost underwent a remarkable turn when He discovered His destiny from the Scriptures. "And he came to Nazareth, where he had been brought up: and, as his custom was, he went into the synagogue on the sabbath day, and stood up for to read. And there was delivered unto him the book of the prophet Esaias. And when he had opened the book, he found the place where it was written, The Spirit of the Lord is upon me, because he hath anointed me to preach the gospel to the poor; he hath sent me to heal the brokenhearted, to preach deliverance to the captives, and recovering of sight to the blind, to set at liberty them that are bruised" (Luke 4:16-18, KJV).

The more you read about the Holy Ghost the more you will know Him and the closer you will be to Him.

CHAPTER 17

YOU NEED A REVELATION OF HIM

TO DEVELOP YOUR relationship with the Holy Ghost, you need a revelation of Him.

Revelation

Revelation means to uncover that which is hidden. It's possible to read the Bible and not understand it. The Holy Ghost will have to reveal Himself to you through the Scriptures. Concerning revelation Paul said, " Surely you have heard about the administration of God's grace that was given to me for you, that is, the mystery made known to me by revelation, as I have already written briefly. In reading this, then, you will be able to understand my insight into the mystery of Christ, which was not made known to people in other generations as it has now been revealed by the Spirit to God's holy apostles and prophets" (Ephesians 3:2-5).

Jesus' Spiritual Identity Revealed

One day the spiritual identity of Jesus was supernaturally revealed to Him. Jesus asked Peter who he thought He was, "He saith unto them, But whom say ye that I am? And Simon Peter answered and said, Thou art the Christ, the Son of the living God. And Jesus answered and said unto him, Blessed art thou, Simon Barjona: for flesh and blood hath not revealed it unto thee, but my Father which is in heaven" (Matthew 16:15-17, KJV). Peter knew the identity of Jesus mentally, but on that day the Holy Ghost revealed His spiritual identity to him. Your spirit can know and understand things your mind has no idea about.

I Still Get Revelations

Till today I still get revelations about the Holy Ghost that I did not know before. One day I was reading my Bible when I came across this Scripture, "When you send your Spirit, they are created, and you renew the face of the ground" (Psalm 104:30).

Three things were revealed to me. First of all, the Holy Spirit can create new body parts for people who are sick because He can "create." Secondly, He can repair malfunctioning body parts. This is because He "renews" or makes new again. Thirdly, the Holy Ghost can deliver a new body part to you. "He sends forth" means He also offers delivery services.

The manufacturer of a car can repair or replace a part with a brand new one. They can also deliver the part to you. God, who created us, can do all that. This revelation increased my faith in creative miracles. Based on this I believed God could heal sickle cell anemia through a creative miracle.

Healed of Sickle Cell Anemia

I know someone who was healed of sickle cell disease. Sometime back someone called me on my phone with an urgent request. He was sickling positive and needed a creative miracle because it cannot be cured. Armed with this revelation I told him God would heal him. At that time I was shopping in a mall, but I paused and prayed in faith.

After about two years he wrote me and shared his testimony with me. He told me after my prayer his skin changed and became like the skin of a newborn baby for a while. That day he was healed instantly. He later did a test and discovered he had become sickling negative. He waited two years because he wanted to make sure of his testimony. We serve a healing Jesus!

That's why we need revelation. Paul said, "The person without the Spirit does not accept the things that come from the Spirit of God but considers them foolishness, and cannot understand them because they are discerned only through the Spirit" (1 Corinthians 2:14).

"However, as it is written: 'What no eye has seen, what no ear has heard, and what no human mind has conceived'—the things God has prepared for those who love him—these are the things God has revealed to us by his Spirit. The Spirit searches all things, even the deep things of God" (1 Corinthians 2:9-10).

How Can You Have Revelations About the Holy Spirit?

Let me share with you a few secrets.

1. You Must Fear Him

Revelation is given to those who fear the Lord. "The LORD confides in those who fear him; he makes his covenant known to them" (Psalm 25:14). In other words, the fear of the Lord will give you revelation concerning the Bible: The Old and New Covenant or Testament.

What Does It Mean to Fear God?

Is it just an emotion? It is more than that? It means to be obedient to God. Moses told Israel, "And now, Israel, what does the LORD your God ask of you but to fear the LORD your God, to walk in obedience to him, to love him, to serve the LORD your God with all your heart and with all your soul" (Deuteronomy 10:12).

He said to fear the Lord by walking in obedience to Him.

2. Pray for Revelation

Paul prayed for the Church of Ephesus to have revelation. He said, "I keep asking that the God of our Lord Jesus Christ, the glorious Father, may give you the Spirit of wisdom and revelation, so that you may know him better" (Ephesians 1:17).

Start praying for revelation and the Holy Ghost will begin to reveal Himself to you.

CHAPTER 18

YOU MUST HAVE THE SAME NATURE

TO DEVELOP YOUR relationship with the Holy Ghost, you must have the same nature as Him.

Your Friends and Your Character

Show me your friend and I will show you your character. There is a cliché that says birds of the same feather or nature flock together. In other words, people tend to hang out with people who are like them. That's why the best friend of a pig is not a bird but a fellow pig. Most of my friends are pastors and this is because I am a pastor myself.

The Holy Ghost's Nature

What is the essential nature of the Holy Ghost? His name has a prefix: holy. That's His essential nature. To be His friend you must have His nature. You must be holy because God is holy.

Jesus attracted the Holy Ghost because of His nature. Before Jesus started His ministry His cousin, John the Baptist, was already a big-time minister who was attracting huge crowds to his meetings. One day he saw Jesus coming towards him and this is what happened. "The next day John saw Jesus coming toward him and said, 'Look, the Lamb of God, who takes away the sin of the world! This is the one I meant when I said, "A man who comes after me has surpassed me because he was before me." I myself did not know him, but the reason I came baptizing with water was that he might be revealed to Israel.' Then John gave this testimony: 'I saw the Spirit come down from heaven as a dove and remain on him' " (John 1:29-32).

John "saw the Spirit come down from heaven as a dove and remain on him." Why was He the only one who attracted the Spirit? Because He was holy. He had the nature of the Lamb. The lamb nature attracts the Holy Spirit.

John had a revelation and saw Jesus as a lamb. This is what he saw. "Then I saw a Lamb, looking as if it had been slain, standing at the center of the throne, encircled by the four living creatures and the elders. The Lamb had seven horns and seven eyes, which are the seven spirits of God sent out into all the earth" (Revelation 5:6). What is the lamb nature?

The Lamb Is a Symbol of Holiness

The word holy means to be set apart for God's use. Recently I made a reservation in a restaurant with some friends of mine. When we arrived a table had been reserved specially for our use. The restaurant was full but our reserved seats were empty. We were the only ones who could sit there.

When we reserve ourselves for the use of the Holy Spirit, only He can use our body, mind, will, emotions, and spirit. "Do not offer any part of yourself to sin as an instrument of wickedness, but rather offer yourselves to God as those who have been brought from death to life; and offer every part of yourself to him as an instrument of righteousness. For sin shall no longer be your master, because you are not under the law, but under grace" (Romans 6:13-14).

I Have Tried to Be Holy

I have been married for almost thirty years, and throughout this period, through God's grace, I have reserved myself only for my wife because that's how God wants me to use my body. I don't expose my eyes to pornography because the Holy Ghost doesn't like it. "I made a covenant with my eyes not to look lustfully at a young woman" (Job 31:1).

I have tried to keep a heart free of bitterness and strife because the Lord does not want my heart to be a garbage bin for negative emotions. The Scripture says, "And do not grieve the Holy Spirit of God, with whom you were sealed for the day of redemption. Get rid of all bitterness, rage and anger, brawling and slander, along with every form of malice. Be kind and compassionate to one another, forgiving each other, just as in Christ God forgave you" (Ephesians 4:30-32). Because of this I quickly forgive people because I don't want to "grieve the Holy Ghost."

I don't remember having an overnight grudge or strife with my wife all these years. I try to keep a good relationship with the Holy Ghost. It's easy to preach and be filled with bitterness over people who have wronged you one way or the other.

The Lamb Is a Symbol of Sacrifice

When I was in my teens I went to London for a holiday. I started attending a local church on Sundays. I made friends with other teenagers in the church.

One of them, a lovely young girl from France, became my friend. One day she suggested we go to France for a weekend for an all-expenses-paid trip. She was going to pay for everything. All I needed to do was to be present.

It looked tempting and exciting, but I knew I wouldn't return as a holy person. I declined the offer although it was tempting. To do this I had to sacrifice my emotions, and my natural sexual inclinations.

Without sacrifice you cannot be holy. That's why Paul said, "Therefore, I urge you, brothers and sisters, in view of God's mercy, to offer your bodies as a living sacrifice, holy and pleasing to God—this is your true and proper worship" (Romans 12:1).

I want you to notice, sacrifice comes before holiness. Without sacrifice you cannot be holy.

It takes sacrifice to swallow your pride and apologize. It takes sacrifice to forgive. It takes sacrifice to have a successful marital relationship. It takes sacrifice to be a minister. It takes sacrifice to control your anger. Sacrifice is the mother of holiness.

The Lamb Is a Symbol of Humility

As a pastor I counsel people who have marital issues. One day I was talking to a gentleman about marriage and he told me he had more experience in marriage than me because he had been married three times. I told him his negative experiences were proof that he needed counsel.

He called himself a Christian, but he was not humble towards the Word of God. To obey God's voice you must be humble like a sheep, "He guides the humble in what is right and teaches them his way" (Psalm 25:9).

People who think they are wiser than God cannot lead holy lives because they will live in rebellion towards God.

CHAPTER 19

YOU MUST SHARE HIS INTERESTS

Common Interests

TO BE A FRIEND of the Holy Ghost you must share the same interests. Interest is the glue that can bind people together. I used to play golf sometime ago but I stopped playing because I developed a back problem. Because of my interest in golf I joined a golf club and made friends with many golfers because of the common interest we shared. Since I stopped playing golf all my golf buddies are no longer my buddies because we don't share the same interest anymore.

I have always been interested in the ministry and because of that many of my friends are ministers. My roommate in college was called Sam. I became interested in him when a mutual friend of ours told me about him. She told me he was spiritual and intelligent and was also coming to study architecture. My interest was peaked and we became friends. Now we both are pastors and remain very good friends. This is because we both share an interest in serving the Lord.

Share His Interests

The Holy Ghost can be a good friend of yours if you share His interests. What is His main interest? Jesus stated His main interest when the Holy Ghost came upon Him. He said, "The Spirit of the Lord is on me, because he has anointed me to proclaim good news to the poor. He has sent me to proclaim freedom for the prisoners and recovery of sight for the blind, to set the oppressed free, to proclaim the year of the Lord's favor" (Luke 4:18-19).

"Because" means this is the reason. The main reason why the Holy Ghost will be close to you is because you have an interest in preaching the Gospel or ministry.

Jesus promised His disciples the Holy Ghost if they would be witnesses. He said, "But you will receive power when the Holy Spirit comes on you; and you will be my witnesses in Jerusalem, and in all Judea and Samaria, and to the ends of the earth" (Acts 1:8).

When the Holy Ghost arrived on the day of Pentecost the first thing He did was to use Peter to preach. "When the people heard this, they were cut to the heart and said to Peter and the other apostles, 'Brothers, what shall we do?' Peter replied, 'Repent and be baptized, every one of you, in the name of Jesus Christ for the forgiveness of your sins. And you will receive the gift of the Holy Spirit. The promise is for you and your children and for all who are far off—for all whom the Lord our God will call.' With many other words he warned them; and he pleaded with them, 'Save yourselves from this corrupt generation.' Those who accepted his message were baptized, and about three thousand were added to their number that day" (Acts 2:37-41).

Soul winning is the supreme interest of the Holy Ghost. Paul reminded Timothy why Christ came into the world, "Here is a trustworthy saying that deserves full acceptance: Christ Jesus came into the world to save sinners—of whom I am the worst" (1 Timothy 1:15).

CHAPTER 20

YOU NEED THE GIFTS OF THE SPIRIT

TO EXPERIENCE THE POWER of the Holy Ghost, you need the gifts of the Spirit.

Power and the Gifts

I have a prepaid electricity meter in my house and sometimes I only realize I have run out of power when my coffee maker refuses to work. Then it dawns on me that I have run out of power. Electrical power in a building isn't manifested to the physical eye till it powers an appliance. The power is manifested by the appliance. For example, you can charge your phone, cook, watch TV, etc. It's a symbiotic relationship because they depend on each other.

You can have all the appliances: a microwave, fridge, computer, etc., but if there is no power they are virtually useless. You can also have electrical power, but if there is no appliance, you cannot manifest or use the power.

The Holy Ghost Is the Power

Until the Holy Ghost powers the gifts of the Spirit, they will be inactive. That's why Jesus said, "But you will receive power when the Holy Spirit comes on you; and you will be my witnesses in Jerusalem, and in all Judea and Samaria, and to the ends of the earth" (Acts 1:8). His presence generates the power and the power activates the gifts of the Spirit.

The Gifts of the Spirit Are the Appliances

"Now about the gifts of the Spirit, brothers and sisters, I do not want you to be uninformed. You know that when you were pagans, somehow or other you were influenced and led astray to mute idols. Therefore I want you to know that no one who is speaking by the Spirit of God says, 'Jesus be cursed,' and no one can say, 'Jesus is Lord,' except by the Holy Spirit.

There are different kinds of gifts, but the same Spirit distributes them. There are different kinds of service, but the same Lord. There are different kinds of working, but in all of them and in everyone it is the same God at work.

Now to each one the manifestation of the Spirit is given for the common good. To one there is given through the Spirit a message of wisdom, to another a message of knowledge by means of the same Spirit, to another faith by the same Spirit, to another gifts of healing by that one Spirit, to another miraculous powers, to another prophecy, to another distinguishing between spirits, to another speaking in different kinds of tongues, and to still another the interpretation of tongues. All these are the work of one and the same Spirit, and he distributes them to each one, just as he determines" (1 Corinthians 12:1-11).

Led Astray to Mute Idols

I want to make an observation. Without the power and gifts of the Holy Spirit, Christians can be attracted to alternative forms of power. Idols, cults, psychics, witchcraft, or even political power. That's why Paul said, "you were influenced and led astray to mute idols" (1 Corinthians 12:2).

I once knew a woman who was a member of my church. Her husband was also a member of one of those large, traditional denominations. One day the husband became sick and was bedridden. She asked me to come and pray for him. One of my spiritual gifts is the gift of healing, so I prayed that the Holy Ghost would manifest His power through the gift and the name of Jesus.

When I started praying the Holy Ghost spoke to me and said He would not answer my prayer. I asked why, and He said the man had three idols under his bed, so He wouldn't. I paused and asked the man if this was true and he confirmed it to be so. I told him he had to destroy the idols if he wanted to be healed.

He allowed me to destroy two of them but he refused to destroy the last one. He said that idol had protected him all his life. Because he refused I couldn't pray for him. He died shortly after that. Although he was a religious man he put his trust in idols because he knew nothing about the power and gifts of the Spirit. He resorted to another form of power.

Four Classifications of Gifts
The gifts of the Spirit can be classified into four sections;

- The Mental Gifts – These give you supernatural mental abilities.
- The Power or Doing Gifts – These help you to do things supernaturally.
- The Seeing Gifts – These give you supernatural sight.
- The Speaking Gifts – These help you to speak to men and God.

Let's examine them closely.

The Mental Gifts
The word of wisdom and the word of knowledge relate to your mental faculties. The word of wisdom is wisdom supernaturally given by the Holy Ghost.

1. The word of wisdom helps you to solve problems supernaturally.
King Solomon was able to solve the complex problem of determining the rightful mother of a disputed child. Two mothers who had just delivered slept in the same room. The baby of one of the mothers died. The mother whose baby died exchanged her baby with the baby of the other mother and claimed it. In the days of very low medical technology it was difficult to determine whose baby had died. Solomon's solution was, the living baby had to be divided.

"The woman whose son was alive was deeply moved out of love for her son and said to the king, 'Please, my lord, give her the living baby! Don't kill him!' But the other said, 'Neither I nor you shall have him. Cut him in two!' Then the king gave his ruling: 'Give the living baby to the first woman. Do not kill him; she is his mother.' When all Israel heard the verdict the king had given, they held the king in awe, because they saw that he had wisdom from God to administer justice" (1 Kings 3:26-28).

My Marriage and the Word of Wisdom

I married when I was a student so I didn't have much money to organize my wedding. As I was wondering how to foot some of my bills the Holy Ghost gave me a word of wisdom. He told me to make a list of my needs and a list of my family members and friends who would be willing to help me financially because He said, "He who finds a wife finds what is good and receives favor from the LORD" (Proverbs 18:22). I decided to tap into this favor.

I assigned each bill to specific individuals and asked for their help. They were all eager to help because they were excited I was getting married. That's how I paid my bills—through a word of wisdom. Wisdom directs you to solve problems. "If the iron be blunt, and he do not whet the edge, then must he put to more strength: but wisdom is profitable to direct" (Ecclesiastes 10:10, KJV).

2. The gift of wisdom helps you to achieve or do things.

Solomon achieved great things through wisdom. "When the queen of Sheba saw all the wisdom of Solomon and the palace he had built, the food on his table, the seating of his officials, the attending servants in their robes, his cupbearers, and the burnt offerings he made at the temple of the LORD, she was overwhelmed" (1 Kings 10:4-5).

The Word of Knowledge

This is the ability to know things by supernatural means.

Sometime ago a man came to see me in my office. As we were speaking I had a vision of him standing in the desert by a broken-down vehicle. He was shocked and told he me three days before he had been driving through the Libyan desert and his car broke down. God gave me this information supernaturally.

When this gift is at work, God shares minute particles of His knowledge with you. David described the extent of God's supernatural knowledge. He said, "Such knowledge is too wonderful for me, too lofty for me to attain. Where can I go from your Spirit? Where can I flee from your presence? If I go up to the heavens, you are there; if I make my bed in the depths, you are there. If I rise on the wings of the dawn, if I settle on the far side of the sea, even there your hand will guide me, your right hand will hold me fast.

"If I say, 'Surely the darkness will hide me and the light become night around me,' even the darkness will not be dark to you; the night will shine like the day, for darkness is as light to you. For you created my inmost being; you knit me together in my mother's womb" (Psalm 139:6-1).

In essence, he said God knows what's happening in heaven, hell, the furthest countries, or ends of the earth, the sea, what happens in darkness, in the light, the past, the present, and eternity. He even knew us before we were conceived in the womb. That's supernatural knowledge.

Jesus knew Peter would betray Him before Peter himself knew it. He said to Simon, "Simon, Simon, Satan has asked to sift all of you as wheat. But I have prayed for you, Simon, that your faith may not fail. And when you have turned back, strengthen your brothers" (Luke 22:31-32). He had already taken preemptive measures by praying for him.

The Word of Knowledge Can Be Used for Business

One day Peter fished all night and caught nothing. Jesus, who was a carpenter with no fishing skills, knew where the fishes were. He directed Peter to a particular spot, "Simon answered, 'Master, we've worked hard all night and haven't caught anything. But because you say so, I will let down the nets.' When they had done so, they caught such a large number of fish that their nets began to break" (Luke 5:5-6). The word of knowledge transformed a failing business into a profitable one.

The Gifts of Power

The gifts of power are the gifts of faith, healing, and working of miracles.

The Gift of Faith

There is a type of faith, which is supernatural. When this gift is in operation God gives you little particles of His own faith to believe Him for the impossible. Jesus did many miracles, which wowed the disciples, "And the apostles said unto the Lord, Increase our faith. And the Lord said, If ye had faith as a grain of mustard seed, ye might say unto this sycamine tree, Be thou plucked up by the root, and be thou planted in the sea; and it should obey you" (Luke 17:5-6, KJV).

Jesus said what they needed was tiny particles of faith; about the size of a mustard seed, which is very tiny. This represents particles of God's own faith, which can be given as a gift. It can move mountains.

A Little Boy Returned to Life

I remember once praying over the phone for a little boy who had died. After about five minutes his dad called me back and said his son had resurrected from the dead. I received the gift of faith at that instant to believe God for the impossible.

Consider how Jesus raised Lazarus from the dead. Martha, the sister of Lazarus, doubted whether Lazarus could rise from the dead. She told Jesus he had been dead four days.

"Then Jesus said, 'Did I not tell you that if you believe, you will see the glory of God?' So they took away the stone. Then Jesus looked up and said, 'Father, I thank you that you have heard me. I knew that you always hear me, but I said this for the benefit of the people standing here, that they may believe that you sent me.' When he had said this, Jesus called in a loud voice, 'Lazarus, come out!' The dead man came out, his hands and feet wrapped with strips of linen, and a cloth around his face. Jesus said to them, 'Take off the grave clothes and let him go.' " (John 11:40-44).

Healing the Sick Miraculously through Prayer

Years ago I was praying at dawn when the power of God struck me to the ground. Suddenly I felt a great warmth on my hands as if my hands were suspended over fire. I asked the Holy Ghost, "What is this?" And He said, "It's the manifestation of the gift of healing." Since then I have seen the Lord heal many people through my prayer.

Jesus Appeared to a Sick Woman

One day a woman suffering from a terrible heart condition sent me a message from the hospital. According to her the Lord appeared to her the previous night and told her to send for me. She didn't know me but the Lord told her my name and how to locate me. The Lord told her He would heal her if I were to come and pray for her.

When I received the message I decided to visit her at the hospital. I drove for four hours to see her because I was in another city. When I entered her ward I was wondering how I would be able to locate her because I had no idea what she looked like.

A woman rose up to meet me and mentioned my name. She said, "I was the one who sent for you." I asked her how she was able to recognize me, and she told me Jesus showed her my picture. I was so excited to learn Jesus had a picture of me! I asked her to repeat that part.

I prayed for the sick woman on Saturday. On Monday she was taken to do further tests and scans. Her heart had become normal so she was discharged. What a powerful healing! If you are believing God to be healed, receive a miracle, in Jesus' name.

Working Miracles through the Power of the Holy Ghost

The gift of miracles has to do with any miraculous answers to prayer, irrespective of what it is. God has used me to pray for people suffering from cancer, and I have seen them recover.

Miracles of Restoration

I have seen miracles of restoration. Thieves once broke into my church member's house and made away with money and his briefcase containing all his valuable documents. His worry was not about the money but the documents. I prayed for him that God would miraculously retrieve and return the documents. That evening when he got home his briefcase had been returned by the thieves. It was standing in front of his door. That was the gift of miracles at work.

Paul worked many miracles. "God did extraordinary miracles through Paul, so that even handkerchiefs and aprons that had touched him were taken to the sick, and their illnesses were cured and the evil spirits left them" (Acts 19:11-12).

The Seeing Gifts

The Gift of Discernment

Spiritual things and spirits cannot be seen with the normal eye, but with this gift your spiritual eye can see them. You can see all kinds of spirits: people's spirits, angels, demons, the Holy Spirit, etc. I have seen Jesus about five times in my lifetime.

The Spirit of Death Retreats

When I was in college, one morning I was sitting on my bed singing a worship song and praying when I heard a knock at the door. I said, "Come in," and to my surprise, Jesus walked in! I said, "Jesus!" in disbelief, and He smiled. He told me to fast and pray concerning the spirit of death, which had taken residence in our residential facility. Every semester a student died in our hall of residence. That was when I came to understand that spirits could inhabit buildings. I fasted and prayed three days, according to His instructions, and the deaths ceased. This gift detected the Spirit of Jesus and the evil spirit in the hall of residence.

Healed from Schizophrenia

At another time I was praying with some friends for a woman suffering from schizophrenia and we seemed to be making no progress. The evil spirit was just laughing and giggling. At a point I fell into a trance. (This means my natural senses were suspended and I was 100 percent in the Spirit realm.)

In the Spirit I saw the woman bound with chains under a river and guarded by an evil spirit. I commanded the spirit to leave her. She screamed in terror and fell down unconscious for about fifteen minutes. When she awoke she was completely delivered and healed. It was through discernment that I was able to see into the spirit realm.

The Speaking or Vocal Gifts

The vocal gifts are expressed through the mouth. They are tongues, interpretation of tongues, and prophecy.

The Gift of Tongues

One of the difficulties of praying is what to say. This deficiency is solved by the gift of speaking in tongues. Paul said, "For if I pray in a tongue, my spirit prays, but my mind is unfruitful" (1 Corinthians 14:14).

Our spirit man prays without depending on the mind. This tends to make prayer easy. You can learn, cook, exercise, and even pray because it doesn't require your mind. "In the same way, the Spirit helps us in our weakness. We do not know what we ought to pray for, but the Spirit himself intercedes for us through wordless groans. And he who searches our hearts knows the mind of the Spirit, because the Spirit intercedes for God's people in accordance with the will of God" (Romans 8:26-27).

We have a weakness in prayer, and it's what to say. This weakness is eliminated by speaking in tongues.

Tongues Could Be the Language of Angels or Men

Paul said, "If I speak in the tongues of men or of angels, but do not have love, I am only a resounding gong or a clanging cymbal" (1 Corinthians 13:1). I see clear advantages in this gift as it helps you to pray for a long time.

I can pray for hours in tongues but for a very short time when I am praying with my mind. Praying in tongues also helps you to pray according to the will of God. "The Spirit intercedes for God's people in accordance with the will of God" (Romans 8:27).

The Gift of Interpretation of Tongues

Because tongues could be a foreign language which the believer cannot understand, sometimes it has to be interpreted, especially if it's a message from the Lord. This gift helps you to decipher it.

Paul said, "If anyone speaks in a tongue, two—or at the most three—should speak, one at a time, and someone must interpret. If there is no interpreter, the speaker should keep quiet in the church and speak to himself and to God" (1 Corinthians 14:27-28).

The Gift of Prophecy

The Old Testament prophets prophesied concerning the coming of Christ and salvation. In reference to this Peter said, "Concerning this salvation, the prophets, who spoke of the grace that was to come to you, searched intently and with the greatest care, trying to find out the time and circumstances to which the Spirit of Christ in them was pointing when he predicted the sufferings of the Messiah and the glories that would follow" (1 Peter 1:10-11).

1. Prophecy means to have supernatural knowledge.

The prophets knew supernaturally that Christ would suffer on the cross and bring salvation to many. Isaiah lived about six hundred years before Jesus but knew about the crucifixion of Christ. He said, "Surely he took up our pain and bore our suffering, yet we considered him punished by God, stricken by him, and afflicted" (Isaiah 53:4). That's supernatural knowledge.

I have sometimes known things supernaturally through the gift of prophecy. There are marriages that I knew would fail although they looked blissful at the beginning.

2. Prophecy means to predict the future.

The prophet Isaiah predicted Jesus would suffer. "The Spirit of Christ in them was pointing when he predicted the sufferings of the Messiah" (1 Peter 1:11).

The end product or fruit of this gift is strengthening, encouraging, and comfort. "But the one who prophesies speaks to people for their strengthening, encouraging and comfort" (1 Corinthians 14:3).

If the gift of prophecy is not producing this end product, then it has to be reexamined.

CHAPTER 21

YOU NEED TO FAST AND PRAY

Fasting and Praying Produces Power

TO EXPERIENCE THE MANIFEST power of the Holy Ghost you need to fast and pray. Jesus experienced the power of the Holy Ghost after fasting for forty days and forty nights.

"Jesus, full of the Holy Spirit, left the Jordan and was led by the Spirit into the wilderness, where for forty days he was tempted by the devil. He ate nothing during those days, and at the end of them he was hungry" (Luke 4:1-2). After He ended the fast.

"Jesus returned to Galilee in the power of the Spirit, and news about him spread through the whole countryside" (Luke 4:14).

"They were amazed at his teaching, because his words had authority. In the synagogue there was a man possessed by a demon, an impure spirit. He cried out at the top of his voice 'Go away! What do you want with us, Jesus of Nazareth? Have you come to destroy us? I know who you are—the Holy One of God!' 'Be quiet!' Jesus said sternly. 'Come out of him!' Then the demon threw the man down before them all and came out without injuring him" (Luke 4:32-35).

Jesus was the first person to introduce the casting out of devils in a significant way. Evil spirits started fleeing after He had fasted and prayed.

Fasting Activates the Power of God

Why does fasting activate the power of God? To understand this I want us to begin by explaining the dynamics or driving forces within the Trinity.

There are three members of the Godhead called the Trinity. They are one but also distinct. Human beings are also like that because we are made in the image of God. We are made up of three distinct parts: we are spirit; we have a soul; and we live in a body. These three also form a single person.

The Trinity Releases the Power

The release of the power of God involves all three members of the Godhead. What are their respective roles?

1. The role of the Father is to make His will known.

That's why in the Lord's Prayer, Jesus told His disciples, "After this manner therefore pray ye: Our Father which art in heaven, Hallowed be thy name. Thy kingdom come. Thy will be done in earth, as it is in heaven" (Matthew 6:9-10, KJV). The will of the Father is made known to the Son.

2. The role of the Son is to say what the will of the Father is.

That's why He is also called "the Word" by reason of His function. At creation the Word played a major part by giving voice to the will of the Father. "In the beginning was the Word, and the Word was with God, and the Word was God. The same was in the beginning with God. All things were made by him; and without him was not any thing made that was made" (John 1:1-3, KJV).

3. The role of the Holy Ghost is to carry out the words of the Son.

When the Holy Ghost hears the command of the Word He moves into action by doing what the Word says. That's why He manifests the power of God. The Holy Ghost only responds to the will of the Father and the word of the Son. Check out this Scripture. "Look in the scroll of the LORD and read: None of these will be missing, not one will lack her mate. For it is his mouth that has given the order, and his Spirit will gather them together" (Isaiah 34:16).

The Father wills, the Son speaks the word, and the Holy Ghost moves into action and carries it out with His power.

A Man Healed on the Sabbath

One day Jesus healed a lame man on the Sabbath. This was against the law of Moses. The Pharisees accused Him and questioned why He did it. "Jesus gave them this answer: 'Very truly I tell you, the Son can do nothing by himself; he can do only what he sees his Father doing, because whatever the Father does the Son also does' " (John 5:19).

In summary, He said He was carrying out the will of His Father. The Father expressed His will by showing Him a revelation that He wanted to heal the man. So the Father willed it, the Son spoke, and the Holy Ghost carried out the instruction.

A Blind Man Healed

The Lord healed a blind man in one of my meetings. At that meeting the Lord told me there was a blind man sitting on the last row towards my right at the back of the church. I walked to the last row and asked if there was a blind man sitting there. The blind man arose to his feet and I prayed. His eyes were opened instantly because the power of the Holy Ghost moved into action.

The Father expressed His will to the Son, the Son spoke to the Holy Ghost, the Holy Ghost told me, I spoke the words I heard, and the Holy Ghost moved into action.

Prayer and Fasting

What has all this got to do with prayer and fasting? One thing that prayer and fasting does is that it makes you spiritual and makes you able to hear the voice of the Holy Ghost.

Only spirits can speak to spirits. It's like how only rabbits can speak to fellow rabbits or lions can speak to fellow lions. You cannot hear the voice of the Spirit with your natural senses, and fasting and prayer makes you spiritually sensitive to God's voice.

Paul said: "However, as it is written: 'What no eye has seen, what no ear has heard, and what no human mind has conceived'—the things God has prepared for those who love him—these are the things God has revealed to us by his Spirit.

"The Spirit searches all things, even the deep things of God. For who knows a person's thoughts except their own spirit within them? In the same way no one knows the thoughts of God except the Spirit of God. What we have received is not the spirit of the world, but the Spirit who is from God, so that we may understand what God has freely given us.

"This is what we speak, not in words taught us by human wisdom but in words taught by the Spirit, explaining spiritual realities with Spirit-taught words. The person without the Spirit does not accept the things that come from the Spirit of God but considers them foolishness, and cannot understand them because they are discerned only through the Spirit" (1 Corinthians 2:9-14).

The natural senses cannot know God's plans and provision. " 'What no eye has seen, what no ear has heard, and what no human mind has conceived'—the things God has prepared for those who love him."

To hear the voice of God you must be in the Spirit. "This is what we speak, not in words taught us by human wisdom but in words taught by the Spirit, explaining spiritual realities with Spirit-taught words" (1 Corinthians 2:13).

Prayer and Fasting Help You Hear

Let me give you another example. Phones can only communicate with another phone because they all speak the same "electronic language." To talk to a phone you must be a phone. When you talk with a friend on the phone, the phone converts your voice into an electronic signal, which is transmitted to your friend's phone by a tower. Your friend's phone then converts it from an electronic signal back into your voice. The phones speak "an electronic language" which only phones understand.

The Holy Ghost speaks a spiritual language that only spiritual people can hear. Prayer and fasting make you spiritual and help you hear the voice of the Spirit.

If you can hear the voice of the Holy Ghost you can access the power of the Holy Ghost because you will be acting in accordance with the will of the Father, the command or word of the Son, and the power of the Holy Ghost.

Prayer and Fasting Generate Miracles

On one occasion I pointed to a woman sitting in the congregation and told her I could see an evil spirit like a huge bird standing beside her. The Holy Ghost told me she had been believing God for a child for over twelve years and she could not conceive. He told me to cast out the spirit, pray for her, and she would have a baby. I did what He told me, and the following month she became pregnant for the first time. Praise be to God! I heard the voice of the Spirit because I was in the Spirit. "I was in the Spirit on the Lord's day, and heard behind me a great voice, as of a trumpet" (Revelation 1:10-11, KJV). John heard the voice of God because he was in the Spirit. You must also be in the Spirit to hear the voice of God.

FINAL WORDS

DO YOU WANT TO BE a friend of the Holy Ghost? To do this you must be able to identify Him as the Ghost of Jesus, since you cannot relate to someone you cannot identify. You must also have a strong desire to know Him because He is the custodian of all that God has for you. Desire spiritual gifts, and fast and pray, so that His power will be manifested through you.

Finally, I want to pray with you. I have seen God perform many powerful miracles remotely. Believe that this prayer will catapult you to another level of relationship with the Holy Ghost.

May God give you the hunger, knowledge, revelation, understanding, wisdom, and grace to be a friend of the Holy Ghost. In Jesus' mighty name. Amen.

ABOUT THE AUTHOR
KAKRA BAIDEN

MANY YEARS AGO the Lord Jesus Christ appeared in a vision to Kakra Baiden and called him into the ministry as a prophet, teacher, and miracle worker. He is also known as "the walking Bible" for his supernatural ability to preach and teach the Bible from memory.

Pastor Baiden is an architect by profession and serves as a bishop of the Lighthouse Chapel International denomination. He has trained many pastors and planted many churches within the Lighthouse denomination.

Currently he is the senior pastor of the Morning Star Cathedral, Lighthouse Chapel International, Accra. He is a sought-after revivalist and conference speaker.

He is also the president of Airpower, a ministry through which he touches the world through radio and TV broadcasts, books, CDs, videos, the Internet, and international conferences dubbed "The Airpower Conference." He has ministered the Word on every continent and is also the author of the best-selling book, *Squatters*.

Pastor Baiden is married to Lady Rev. Dr. Ewuradwoa Baiden and they have four children.

For additional information on Kakra Baiden's books
and messages (CDs and DVDs),
write to any of these addresses:

US
26219 Halbrook Glen Lane
Katy, TX 77494

UK
32 Tern Road
Hampton, Hargate
Cambridgeshire
Pe78DG

GHANA
P.O. Box SK 1067
Sakumono Estates, Tema
Ghana-West Africa

E-MAIL: info@kakrabaiden.org
WEBSITE: www.kakrabaiden.org
FACEBOOK: www.facebook.com/KakraBaiden
TWITTER: www.twitter.com/ProphetKakraB

www.ingramcontent.com/pod-product-compliance
Lightning Source LLC
Chambersburg PA
CBHW071630040426
42452CB00009B/1561